Don't Give Up

Trusting God with Your Wandering Loved Ones

Chuck Lawless

Don't Give Up:
Trusting God with Your Wandering Loved Ones

ISBN 979-8-9954034-1-8

Church Answers
Franklin, Tennessee

Printed in the United States of America

CONTENTS

CHAPTER 1

An Introduction and Invitation

> Sometimes you just need to hear your own words. I'm a professor of evangelism who's still learning to lean hard on the Lord on behalf of wanderers I love.

In some ways, I personally needed this book more than any other book I've written.

For that reason, I am asking you to start this book by taking a minute to pray for me and for wandering people I love. I have just paused to pray for you and your wandering loved ones, too, as I write this chapter.

In fact, the topic of prayer will echo throughout this book. It's on our knees that we best trust God and wait for Him to act. Indeed, lying prone before the Father on behalf of our loved ones is not a bad place to begin this book.

I will later invite you into more of the story of why this book is so important to me, but let me give you some personal background first.

The day God saved me when I was 13 years old, I'm convinced He called me to preach. On that day in August of 1974, I sensed clearly in my mind and heart these words: "I want you to preach My Word."

I realize some folks might debate that understanding of my calling, but I can only report what I experienced. You will learn more of my conversion story in the next chapter, but suffice to say that I did not yet have any understanding of a "call" to preach when I turned to Christ as a young teenager. I didn't own my own Bible, nor did I know anything about the Holy Spirit. All I know is that something happened in my heart that day, and those words about preaching the Word have never wavered in my heart in more than 50 years since then.

Within just a few years of my conversion, I was serving as the pastor of a small, struggling, country church in Ohio. Looking back, I realize they just needed a preacher, and they could not afford much; that was okay, though, because I wasn't much anyway—plus, I just wanted to preach even if they never paid me. Those folks, though, grew to love me, and they quickly showed me the beauty of that congregation I was privileged to shepherd. They weren't perfect—and I certainly wasn't—but they were special.

I hadn't officially been a pastor long, however, before I learned stories of folks I call "wandering loved ones" in this book. Some of the wanderers were members of my church's families who had not yet come to know the Lord despite, in many cases, having years of gospel witness around them. It seemed then that some of those wanderers just kept running faster and faster away from the gospel.

Other wanderers had at some point indicated a decision to follow Christ, but they had by that point strayed from that commitment. Some, I'm certain, had never truly followed Christ in the first place—which actually placed them in the wandering group I just described in the previous paragraph. They had gone through the motions of Christianity, but with no real heart change. Their present-tense wandering when I was their pastor was only a symptom of a much deeper need for salvation.

Still others, I believe, had genuinely turned to Christ at some point in their lives. Poor discipleship, though, too often accompanied by very public internal conflict in this little congregation, made them vulnerable to ongoing spiritual struggle. It opened the gate to their wandering. Our theology strongly affirmed the eternal security of genuine believers held in God's hand, but parents and grandparents nevertheless wept often over their wandering loved ones. The contrasts between their past-tense faithfulness and present-tense wandering often produced faith struggles for faithful members of that little church.

> **Wanderers:** not only those who've seemingly walked away from their faith of their upbringing, but also those who've simply never responded positively to the gospel despite years of witness

Little did I know then how often stories like these would mark the lives of Christians I've been privileged to shepherd and walk beside over the years. For example, few things in ministry have been as gut-wrenching to me as praying with senior saints who tearfully and passionately pleaded with God to save their still non-believing adult children before He called the saints home. You'll learn in the next chapter that my story was just the opposite, though no less painful at times: I prayed fervently for years for aging parents and grandparents as I desperately feared they would die without a Savior. When you know your loved one's ongoing wandering will lead only to destruction apart from God's intervention, your heart looks for anything to give you hope.

That's one reason I wrote this book. I want you to be hope-filled if I've described your situation.

Others I've ministered with have offspring they rightly raised, but who now are clearly moving in faulty directions. Fellow pastors I know have experienced that pain when their own children wander. So have missionaries whose adult children not only walk away from faith, but they often do so continents and time zones away from their parents who care so much. Lay leaders in churches sometimes describe the same kind of pain (and, to be frank, some can tell their personal stories that made their own parents pray and grieve over them). Even some of my older students today give me similar descriptions of their teens and college students who've already taken a detour from their upbringing.

Wanderers. They seem to be all around us.

So do those who are waiting for their wanderers to come home, even if they don't always talk openly about their pain.

The stories of wanderers just keep coming, both of those who've never believed and those who say they once believed. And, with the seemingly growing popularity of deconstructing faith, the stories seem to be even more numerous.

I assume you've picked up this book because you or someone you know is dealing with a wandering loved one. If so, I say from the start that I make no claim that reading this small resource will give you simple, quick-fix solutions for changing somebody else's heart. Only God transforms the hearts of wanderers.

Instead, my goal in this book is to offer *you* something for *your* heart. I want you to keep believing, keep praying, keep trusting, and keep looking for the hand of God in your life and in the lives of those you love—even if one of them is wandering in the wilderness somewhere. If you read this book and leave it with a glimmer of increased hope for your wandering loved one, I will be grateful to the Lord.

"Keep believing, keep praying, keep trusting, and keep looking for the hand of God in your life and in the lives of those you love."

These are my own words I need to hear today as I wait for my own wanderers to come home.

Now, I invite you into the rest of this book. I'm guessing that you're a busy person who does not have significant time set aside to read. If so, I've tried to make this book concise, practical, and encouraging. You can likely read a chapter, make a few notes, consider some action steps, and say a prayer in a single setting.

At the risk of giving too much away in this introductory chapter, here are some of my goals for you as we journey together in this reading:

1. You will remember again just how important prayer is in this task.

2. You will find renewed hope and faith in the task of waiting on God.

3. You will recognize the enemy's arrows of discouragement as you intercede for others.

4. You will learn to grieve for others even when they don't grieve for themselves.

5. You will see God's hand in the glimpses of His work around you.

6. You will love others even when they're unlovable as you seek to take the gospel to them.

7. You will act on challenges to take practical steps based on this book.

8. You will look forward in faith to the day when your wandering loved one will come home.

Because I want you to do more than simply read this book, every chapter finishes with a few practical, personal action steps to consider based on that chapter's content. Included among those steps is an opportunity to state a primary insight you want to remember from each chapter.

I encourage you *not* to simply skim those action steps as if they don't matter. Think about them. Pray about them.

Discuss them with your spouse or another trusted friend. Review each previous chapter's steps as a way to reinforce your reading before you begin each new chapter.

And, as important as anything you do, pray *before* you read each chapter.

Then, pray some more ***as*** **you read**.

Pray, too, ***after*** **you've read** as you think about the action steps.

Then, start the prayer process again before you read the next chapter. I assure you this practice of prayer will make sense as you read this book. In fact, I invite you to take time again right now to pray for your reading and for wanderers who come to mind as you work through this book.

Thank you, friend, for joining me on this brief journey. I've been praying that God will use this resource in some way to call a wanderer back to Him. Perhaps that returning wanderer will be someone you love. Maybe it will be someone I love. Or, maybe both of us will see a miracle.

May the God who captured us in our own wandering be pleased as we intercede for others and watch for Him to work in their lives.

ACTION STEPS:

1. Spend time in prayer based on what you've read. Pray especially for someone you love who is wandering.

2. Thank God for calling you to Himself when He saved you. Ask Him to help you follow Him fully for the rest of your life.

3. State for yourself (even write somewhere) the primary insight you've gained from this chapter.

CHAPTER 2

Why Not Just Give Up?

I heard the same story again this week. This time, I heard it from the lips of a Christian believer whose adult daughter, raised under a strong Christian witness and once a self-professed faithful follower of Jesus herself, had seemingly defected from the faith of her childhood. No longer does she exhibit any sense of passion for Jesus. In fact, she almost vehemently denies any connection with Christianity.

Right now, all her parents can do is pray . . . and weep.

To be truthful, they weep over their daughter's sins much more than she does over her own. Their other adult children also grieve their sister's choices. It just hurts as all of them weep and wait.

At the same time, I've heard similar stories from believers whose older parents do not yet believe. These believers love their parents—often *really good* parents in the world's eyes—and they long for them to know Jesus. The older their parents get, in fact, the greater their burden becomes. None of us has forever to decide to be a Christ-follower.

And, once again, all these believing children can do is pray, weep. . . and wait. I know, because I've been there. I've been on my knees in that situation.

My guess is, in fact, that you've picked up this book because you're facing a similar kind of anguish over a loved one. You're struggling, and you're looking for hope. If that's the case, I remind you again that I've written this book with that goal in mind: to give you hope. You really can't just give up.

The Power of Prayer

I realize that my statements above, "all they can do is pray" suggest that somehow prayer is a last recourse that may or may not be effective. If you know me at all, you know that's not what I believe.

In fact, my own salvation is the result not only of a friend repeatedly sharing the gospel with me, but also of his mother and grandmother joining him in prayer after I had continually rejected his message. To be honest, I don't know why my seventh-grade classmate and his family didn't give on me. I probably would have given up on him if the situation had been reversed at the time.

I was a 12-year-old brat, not having been raised in a Christian home and having no knowledge whatsoever about the gospel. Had you asked me at the time who Adam and Eve were, I couldn't have told you. I had never even seen a Bible up close . . . that was, until I met Randy, my classmate. Even then, it would be months after the first gospel conversation that I would see a Bible.

Randy was a fanatic for Jesus who wanted me to know Him, too, and he told me about Christ *every day* of my seventh-grade year. He was pushy at times, so much so that I occasionally pretended to be sick to avoid going to school that day. I figured if I could avoid Randy, I could also avoid any conviction (though I didn't know the term at that time) about following Jesus. The fact that I'm writing this book right now is evidence that I was wrong.

Randy simply didn't give up on me. He just kept speaking to me . . . challenging me . . . and praying for me the best way a 12-year-old believer could. More importantly, God didn't give up on me. He knew exactly what I needed to convince me to eventually respond to His wooing grace. The sovereign ruler of the universe knew I needed a gospel witness-friend who would keep pursuing me as fast as I was running. I needed a God-focused young, fervent evangelist to keep proclaiming the good news to me.

I survived seventh grade, though, without becoming a Christian. I was sure that when I didn't have to face Randy every day, I wouldn't have to battle him anymore. I had won that struggle—or so I thought—when our summer break came that year. What I didn't know was that Randy and his family cranked up their praying for me that summer. Their behind-the-scenes praying about which I knew nothing would change my life.

It was, in fact, during that summer break between my seventh and eighth-grade years that I finally made my way to church for the first time in my life. To be candid, I went simply so I could say to Randy when eighth-grade classes started again, "I went to church a few weeks ago, so stay off my back!" Little did I know that God would grab my heart at church that day, make me His child, and alter the rest of my life after on my faith response to Him at age 13. Randy never gave up on me, and God never ignored Randy's evangelistic efforts and prayers on my behalf.

The day God saved me, my pastor (whose title I didn't know then) told me to start telling others about Jesus and begin praying for them to know Jesus, too. I didn't know how to do either one, but I gave them my best shot. What I did was tell others about Jesus with the same zeal (and occasional obnoxiousness) that I saw in Randy.

I was so excited about following Jesus that I was certain everyone would hear me right away. I was sure no one would ignore or reject my words as I had done toward Randy. After all, how could anyone not want forgiveness, peace, eternal life, and Christian friends who would become family? Why would they *not* want joy that would give them glee in the day and sweet rest at night?

It didn't take me long, though, to realize that not everyone wanted to listen. Especially my family. And often my friends, too.

I would have to learn not to give up.

The Need for Patience and Persistence (and the Rest of This Book)

I know that my mom and dad loved our family the best way they knew to do so, and they provided for us with a deep work ethic even if they didn't always demonstrably show us love. Our home was hardly healthy, however. I still remember with pain my dad's oft-violent displays of anger and my mom's resultant tears of fear. As the oldest son, I lived with a sense of responsibility to protect Mom despite my own fear of my dad. I can still see in my mind the dents in the walls of our home where my dad threw objects in anger. Maybe you have a similar story.

You can imagine how much my Christian conversion affected me in that context. I found in Christ and in His followers a love I had never known. The church building became a "safe place" for me, so I was seldom absent any time the church doors were opened. Nobody was hollering there, and everyone seemed to live with an unusual peace there. I would learn later, of course, that church folks can also be angry and divisive, but that's not what I experienced when I first became a believer.

My parents were not opposed to my Christianity, but nor were they overjoyed by it. They realized that my church family was increasingly important to me, especially after I was old enough to drive to church activities. Neither was interested in listening when I tried to share the gospel with them. I would later learn that my dad was at the time a pluralist (believing there are multiple ways to God) and my mom could not believe that God would truly forgive her when she had lived a lifetime of rebellion.

So, I began praying for them . . . and praying some more for them . . . and some more. For years, in fact. For more than five years. More than 10 years. More than 15 years. More than 20. More than 25.

I and others prayed for more than 30 years for my parents with no results.

And, along the way, why would I not just give up at some point? After a while, what's the point of praying and hoping any longer? I would not be truthful with you if I said I never doubted that God would save my parents.

> Even if you're doubting God today, I'm praying that you do not give up. He is still a saving God.

I trust that the rest of this book, though, including the remainder of my parents' story (which I assume you can guess even this early in this book) will say to you: "Here's why you can't give up." I pray that as you read, you will learn to be prayerful, persistent, patient, and praise-filled as you wait for a loved one to come home:

- *prayerful*, meaning you're staying on your knees
- *patient*, meaning you're trusting God's timing
- *persistent*, meaning you're pressing on and not giving up
- *praise-filled*, meaning you're keeping your eyes on God who is bigger than anything you face.

That's where I want your heart to be even as you wait for a wanderer to come home. I, too, want my heart to be there on behalf of my wandering loved ones as I write this book: prayerful, persistent, patient, and praise-filled. With that goal in mind, let's continue this journey toward hope together!

ACTION STEPS:

1. Think about God's patient grace toward you before you became a believer. Trust Him to save others you love.

2. Of these characteristics—prayerful, patient, persistent, and praise-filled—identify the one where you most need to grow. Ask the Lord for His help.

3. State for yourself (even write somewhere) the primary insight you've gained from this chapter.

CHAPTER 3

Why It's So Hard to Reach People (and Keep Praying when We Don't)

This book is not only about being prayerful, patient, persistent, and praise-filled; it's also about being obedient. It's about our responsibility to evangelize others and pray for them. If we never tell the gospel to others in the first place, we probably wouldn't be meeting via this resource to talk about not giving up.

Let me go back to my story. I wish I could say that I found it easy to share the gospel with my parents. Indeed, I wish I could say that evangelism is just easy for me in general. After all, I'm serving as a Senior Professor of Evangelism and Missions as I write this book. I would be less than truthful, though, if I tried to convince you in this chapter just how easy evangelism is—especially when you're trying to evangelize family members who know you best.

Why Evangelism Can be Hard

Evangelism is hard for many believers. Sometimes fear stops them from speaking the good news. Most believers have no strongly evangelistic role models. Many have never been trained in evangelism in the first place. Some Christians are also simply apathetic about the lost. Perhaps some of these reasons I personally find evangelism difficult will resonate with you, too, as we think about this topic:

1. **I live in a Christian bubble.** Much of my life is hanging out with other Christians. It's not easy to evangelize when you don't have friendships with non-believers.

2. **As a pastor, it's easy to equate my pulpit ministry or my missions work with doing evangelism.** When I preach the gospel every Sunday, it doesn't take long to convince myself that I don't need to do more evangelism. When I travel overseas to tell others

about Jesus, I can also let myself off the evangelistic hook for a while after the trip.

3. **I sometimes take Jesus for granted.** I wrote the book *Nobodies for Jesus* to address this issue, but I've learned that fighting against this tendency is a day-by-day, moment-by-moment work.[1] None of us defaults into godly wonder that leads to talking about Jesus.

4. **I'm so busy it's hard to find time to be with lost people—or actually, people in general.** I work more than one job—all that are ministry-related. What I must admit now is that I can allow ministry busyness to get in the way of knowing people who need Jesus.

5. **I forget about the reality of hell.** Very early in my pastoral ministry, God broke me over the death of a non-believing friend. That event took place a long time ago. Too long ago, apparently, since I needed this reminder today.

6. **I'm naturally introverted.** I'm not the one to begin most conversations. My natural tendency is to wait

until someone else starts the conversation—and non-believers seldom do that!

7. **I don't have enough prayer warriors praying Ephesians 6:18-20 and Colossians 4:2-4 for me.** If the apostle Paul needed believers asking the Lord to give him opportunity, boldness, and clarity in sharing, I surely do, too—so much so that I will come back to these verses later in this study. My guess is that you need that kind of prayer support, too, as you evangelize.

8. **I'm trying to reach people *who are lost*.** They are dead in their sin (Eph 2:1). Their hearts are hardened. They can't save themselves, and nor can I save them. I face an impossible task in my own power.

An Even Bigger Reason that Evangelism is Hard

In the rest of this chapter, I want to talk about another hindrance to evangelism we seldom consider: a supernatural enemy who fights against us if we seek to share the good news.

Think about it this way. The Bible is clear about the condition of non-believers, and its writers often speak of lostness in terms of spiritual conflict. The apostle Paul particularly uses this imagery:

- **Ephesians 2:2** (NLT) – "You used to live in sin, just like the rest of the world, obeying the devil—the commander of the powers in the unseen world. He is the spirit at work in the hearts of those who refuse to obey God."

- **2 Corinthians 4:3-4** – "If the Good News we preach is hidden behind a veil, it is hidden only from people who are perishing. Satan, who is the god of this world, has blinded the minds of those who don't believe."

- **Colossians 1:13-14** – "For he has rescued us from the kingdom of darkness and transferred us into the Kingdom of his dear Son, who purchased our freedom and forgave our sins."

- **2 Timothy 2:26** – "Then they will come to their senses and escape from the devil's trap. For they have been held captive by him to do whatever he wants."

- **Acts 26:17b-18a** – "Yes, I am sending you [the Apostle Paul] to the Gentiles to open their eyes, so they may turn from darkness to light and from the power of Satan to God."

Following the powers of the unseen world . . . blinded by Satan . . . living in the kingdom of darkness . . . held in the devil's trap . . . under the power of Satan—these statements describe the people we're trying to reach (including our loved ones), and it shouldn't surprise us that the enemy fights back against us when we seek to introduce non-believers to Christ. We shouldn't be shocked when he pushes us toward discouragement when our waiting for others to come to Christ seems far too long.

I describe this reality with these words in my book, *The Battle is Not Mine*:

> He [Satan] doesn't need to aim at non-believers because they are already in his kingdom. They are following the "ruler of the air" (Eph 2:2, CSB), blinded by the god of this age (2 Cor 4:3-4), living in the domain of darkness (Col 1:13), caught in the devil's trap (2 Tim 2:26), and under the power of Satan (Acts 26:18). These are tough words to accept when we have loved ones who aren't Christ-followers, but

> the words are the Word of God. The enemy has little reason to aim at folks already in darkness. Instead, he targets believers because we are God's plan to take the gospel to our neighbors and the nations.[2]

The enemy comes after us in so many ways. He wants us living in sin so our lifestyle contradicts our message. He promotes false teaching that keeps us from evangelizing at all. He delights in church division that distracts us from doing gospel-sharing. And, as I wrote in a previous paragraph, he comes after us with discouragement when we actually do evangelism but see no results. As gospel witnesses, you and I wear a bullseye on our back for the enemy when we evangelize.

Simply put, the enemy comes after us when we share the good news. That's one reason—a reason we think about too little—that evangelism is hard. The enemy also attacks the prayer warrior who has shared the gospel with a loved one, but who, like the father of the prodigal son in Luke 15, remains waiting at the end of the driveway for that loved one's return home. Warfare has a way of weakening our resolve to wait in faith.

That spiritual warfare is not the final word, however. Jesus has already defeated the enemy through His cross (Col 2:15). The enemy will ultimately be bound (Rev

20:10). The gospel is still good news, and God is still drawing people to Himself (Rev 7:9). Among those people may well be someone you've been praying for a long time. And, I'm hoping in faith that it might be someone I've been praying for, too.

For sure, God also still welcomes us to come to His presence boldly in prayer (Heb 4:16). His calendar and His clock are not ours—so we must learn to trust Him even in what seems to us to be great delays—but He is always right on time. I've learned over the years, too, that you don't worry much about the delay once God has answered your prayers! The calendar loses its significance when God finally saves someone you love or pulls a wandering believer back home.

> The gospel is still good news, and God is still drawing people to Himself.

You and I still have good news to announce—the good news of a Savior.

We can still do the work of evangelism in the power of the Spirit.

We can also keep praying in faith that God is still working.

And, we can keep watching for our loved ones to come home.

None of these things is really that hard when we put on the full armor of God (Eph 6:10-17) and keep our eyes on our gracious God who is longsuffering and miracle-working. We don't have to let the enemy trample on our heart and rob us of our hope. We *can* still long with faith and trust for the day when we will throw a celebration party because our loved one has come home.

And, in that day, the praises we raise for Him today will be only louder!

> "I can only look forward to the day when my son comes back—and we will celebrate his return without worrying about where he's been."
>
> —a prayerful father waiting for a wandering son

ACTION STEPS:

1. Take some time to review the Bible texts in this chapter. Think about the reality of lostness.

2. Prayerfully make plans to tell somebody about Jesus this week—including your wandering loved one if you have opportunity.

3. State for yourself (even write somewhere) the primary insight you've gained from this chapter.

CHAPTER 4

Learning to Wait

This book is really about waiting on God.

I wish it weren't, though, because I don't like waiting. My wife will tell you that I'm probably the most impatient person she knows. I don't like traffic . . . or restaurant lines . . . or doctor's office delays . . . or church events that unnecessarily start late. I jokingly tell people that I can only hope that we will all go into heaven at the same time . . . .

So, I struggle at times when I've prayed for people for so long that it seems God isn't listening. In those difficult times for me, I'm always reminded to think about reasons God sometimes calls us to wait in the first place.

Why God Calls to Wait

I can't speak for God in explaining every reason He may call us to wait, but here are some things I've learned over the years:

1. **Waiting reminds us that God is in charge.** We're not in charge of the timing of God's work. We don't control all things. Only God does, and His calling us to wait reminds us of that truth.

2. **Waiting teaches us to be patient.** Because of the way I started this chapter, you know I need to learn this lesson. And then learn it again. And again. I don't mind God being my teacher, though, since I know how much He loves me.

3. **Waiting challenges us to look with eyes of faith.** Faith is the evidence of things unseen, the confidence of things not yet taking place (Heb 11:1). The concept almost assumes a gap in timing between our request and God's response. If everything happened immediately, faith would be less necessary—so, for now, we watch and believe.

4. **Waiting reveals our idolatries.** If we simply can't wait on God, it's likely because something we want to happen *according to our timing* is more important to us than God's overall plan. We think our plan is so right that God needs to respond to it right now.

5. **Waiting prepares us for whatever God has for us in the future.** Whatever God's plan is, waiting is often God's way of saying, "You're not ready to receive what you want yet." He knows our hearts, and He alone knows when He needs to do some work in us before granting our request.

6. **Waiting pushes us to trust.** To be honest, this reason is where I most struggle. I'm learning again that it's one thing to teach about trust—but it's another matter entirely to live it out when it's *your* life affected. I need to hear again and again Jesus' words to Jairus after his daughter had died, "Just keep believing" (Mark 5:36)—and then just do it, no matter how long I must wait for an answer.

7. **Waiting encourages us to remember God's blessings in the past.** Recently as I was struggling with waiting as I pray for a wandering friend, my brother—who is a faithful Christ-follower—sent me

this text about his own life when he, too, had been wandering: "Think of the story about your brother, who likely had run farther away from God than any believer ever has . . . [but] God didn't give up on him." I needed that reminder of God's past faithfulness then. I need it again today, too.

8. **Waiting changes us in the process.** We might be waiting for others to change, but God might be working to change us first. He sees the big picture, knows the ultimate plan, and loves all of us. He just might be doing some "meantime" work in our hearts while we're waiting (sometimes impatiently) for Him to work in others.

9. **Waiting reminds us that God is in charge of eternity.** That truth may not sound comforting when we want an answer yesterday, but my point is that our God is in charge of forever. That's one reason why seeming delays that require waiting shouldn't bother us.

> "Waiting for God to answer my prayer isn't like waiting at the doctor's office, a passive state where my mind drifts and I distract myself with magazines or games on my phone. Waiting for God involves deep work in our spirit—one in which we learn about his heart, his grief over sin, his long-suffering nature, his comfort, his faithfulness."
>
> –a hurting, but praying mother waiting for
> a daughter to come home

Why We Must Watch while We Wait

I realize that the story of the prodigal son in Luke 15 is about much more than a waiting father. In fact, it's as much about the older son who reflects the negative and arrogant heart of the Pharisees in Luke 15:1-2 as it is about the father. Nevertheless, I do at times think about what the father in this parable must have felt. I think about mothers, too, who suffer their own kind of anguish over wayward children, but I will focus on fathers for the rest of this chapter as I relate to the father in this parable.

You might think about that father, too, especially if you have a child who has wandered into the far country. Maybe Father's Day is especially tough for you. While others rejoice as they celebrate the holiday, you're more like the father in the parable—likely watching, waiting, surely grieving, hoping . . . and watching and waiting some more.

You did the best you could in raising your children, but at least one has made choices leading only to trouble. Another may have developed a pharisaical attitude like the older brother in the Luke 15 parable. You've been praying, trusting God to draw your wandering child back (and hoping that the return comes sooner than later). Nothing would mean more to you on the next Father's Day than the return of your wanderer—and you're asking God to make that happen.

You've been here before, though. Like last Father's Day. And the Father's Day the year before. And even the year before that one. Nevertheless, you still stand at the end of the driveway and watch for a returning child in the distance. You know it's tough to keep believing, but you also know that giving up hope is to deny the power of God to change your child's heart. So, you pray some more and watch some more and wait some more and then pray some more again.

Let me relate this story to my life a bit more. Pam and I don't have children, so I admit I can't sense all that you're experiencing if your child is wandering. I can, though, argue from a lesser to a greater perspective—that is, I do know what it's like to grieve when some young men Pam and I have loved as sons have wandered farther than I ever thought they would. These guys have been God's special gift to me, and I've wept for years over some of their departures from the faith. I'm sure, though, that my grief has been only a taste of what fathers experience when their own children roam too far.

I remember crying for one "son" when he shared no grief despite the depth of his sin. I longed for him to return when he longed only to avoid those calling him back (including me). Somehow, I felt helpless even when I tried to simply entrust him to God's care. Though the story eventually ended well under God's sovereign "never let go" hand, my heart still tenses a bit today when I remember that anguish. You probably know that feeling even more if your own child has wandered.

I've remembered more than once since then that God keeps His eyes on His children, including those who wander afar. He loves our children more than we ever could. He who died for them continually draws them back to Him; they cannot wander so far that He does not know where they are. We may not always know where our loved ones are, but God does . . . . and that truth ought to give us hope. Just as Jesus kept His eyes on Simon Peter in the apostle's rebellion (Luke 22:61), He knows exactly where our wanderers are.

> "One lesson we've learned in the last few years: we're waiting on the Lord (which brings new strength, Isaiah 40:31), not on the wanderer (which can be exhausting, discouraging, and depressing). Wait on the Lord."
>
> —a helpful word to me from a wise and waiting father

As I've said in a previous chapter, the wait for our wanderers to come home doesn't seem so long when you see them coming around the corner and your heart leaps for joy. The calendar doesn't matter then, and the clock matters only because you want to speed quickly toward the coming reunion. Wanderers who can't hide forever from the wooing love of God may be just around the corner.

So, we watch and wait.

Hurting parent, keep praying, watching, and waiting. Only God knows what's coming.

Loving sister or brother, don't give up on God's work in your sibling's life. God's still saving people.

Despairing child, keep looking in faith as you pray for a grandparent or parent to come to Christ. Wait, but wait in faith.

Faithful husband or wife, keep your eyes on Jesus as you intercede for your non-believing spouse. Wait, but with your focus on the Son.

Don't quit going to the end of the driveway. Don't let the enemy rob you of your hope or turn your heart from God. Instead, trust that in His timing and grace, you will someday see the dust rising as your loved one comes home.

In the meantime, learn what's He teaching you through your waiting period.

ACTION STEPS:

1. Do a Bible study on the word, "wait," to see what you learn.

2. Decide if you are watching and waiting *in faith and hope* for your loved one's return.

3. State for yourself (even write somewhere) the primary insight you've gained from this chapter.

CHAPTER 5

What to Do when You Grieve a Loved One's Sin More than He or She Does

Sometimes the loved one we most want to come to Christ is a good person in the world's eyes. I think of my mom who, as she began to recognize that she was someday going to face eternity, also began to do good for others more than she had ever done. If she could help neighbors, she did. If she found opportunities to "minister" to others (though she would never have used that verb), she took advantage of those opportunities. Those of us who knew her well suspected that she was seeking to earn salvation she could not believe God would simply grant her if she turned from her wrong and trusted Him. The truth of grace was just too much for her to fathom.

On the other hand, sometimes the people for whom we're most praying aren't giving much thought to good works. It might be, in fact, that some aren't thinking about "works" at all since that's a concept from our Christian lingo. They're just living as they wish, without concern for the rightness or wrongness of their actions. "Sin" isn't much an issue for people who aren't worried about being sinners; so, grief over their choices makes little sense to them.

Other wanderers raised in a Christian home understand that Christians would say their choices are in rebellion against their Creator—but they just aren't worried about that thought. Even if their parents were godly examples, they've chosen to ignore or deny the faith of their childhood. As a son once said to me about his own life, they've decided to "live as they want and take their chances with the consequences of their choices." Any grief they have over their actions seems fleeting at best.

They don't grieve much over their lives . . . but you and I do on their behalf. We weep more over their spiritual state than they weep over their own. Their tears seem non-existent, but ours are ongoing and numerous. Our hearts just ache for them.

I assume that someone you know and love fits some description close to one I've portrayed here. If you haven't borne that kind of burden, perhaps you know someone who's shouldering that kind of weight today. And, the day may well come when you also grieve someone's sin more than he or she does. I pray not, but you might be the mother or father of the prodigal someday if you aren't already.

When you do walk in the footsteps of the father of the prodigal son, I encourage you to hang on to these simple instructions—*keep* doing these things:

1. **Keep praying.** It's surely easy to get discouraged when you've prayed and prayed, with no apparent changes in your loved one's life. When you quit praying, though, your silence is a confession that you've given up on somebody—and on God. Prayerlessness leaves wanderers living in sin.

> "Sometimes I have to remind myself of Peter's words to Jesus when I'm tempted to stop praying: 'Lord, to whom will we go? You have the words of eternal life' [John 6:68]. If I don't pray, to whom would I go?"
>
> —a praying father

2. **Keep inviting.** That is, keep inviting others to join you in praying for your wanderer. As we prayed for decades for my dad and mom to follow Christ, I invited others—no matter where I was traveling in the United States or around the world—to join me in praying for them. I'm sure you're not surprised by this point that I believe those united prayers made a difference, as I will show you later in this book.

3. **Keep sharing.** If you're like me, you probably carry burdens far too long on your own before you ask someone to bear them with you. You might even ask others to pray (#2 above), but you do so without genuinely letting others into your pain. Be prayerfully wise and discreet in your choices for "burden bearers," but share your grief over your wanderer. Somebody is ready to walk with you and hold you up.

4. **Keep walking.** Stay faithful yourself. Reject the enemy's arrows that he aims particularly at you. Don't turn in disappointment from God or against Him out of anger. Instead, walk in a manner worthy of your calling as a believer (Eph 4:1). You can't expect God to answer your prayers for somebody else if you're walking in intentional rebellion yourself.

5. **Keep standing.** Here's my point (and it's not an easy one): don't let your wanderer's departure lead you to redefine what is right and wrong. Just recently, I heard about believers who shifted their thinking and rejected the Bible's teaching in order to, in their own words, "love our child." Sin remains sin, however, regardless of how much we love the people living in it.

6. **Keep believing.** I'll say it again: God knows exactly where your loved one is. The One who created our loved ones and died for them still loves them; in fact, He loves our wanderers more than you and I do. His love for them is higher than the skies, deeper than the oceans, and wider than the miles. That "miles" point especially matters when your wanderer is in the distant country.

7. **Keep grieving.** That means your anguish may not go away entirely, but the minute you stop grieving sin is the minute you also start caring less about your wanderer's choices. Agonizing over sin keeps you on your knees—the right place to be on behalf of a wanderer. Just be sure to keep crying out to God in your grief.

8. **Keep loving.** There's a legitimate place at times for church discipline for genuine believers who've wandered, but many wanderers have walked away from the church first because they assumed the church would reject them rather than love them. That conclusion may have been proven wrong in many cases, but the assumptions of wanderers have nevertheless often been heartfelt. Love your wanderer even if others don't seem to—and even if he or she thinks you've lost your love, too.

9. **Keep listening.** Follow the Spirit's guide to know when and how to speak into the situation, but be willing to listen to your wanderer more than you speak at times. You and I have the answer in Jesus, but we usually don't get very far when we browbeat others with our message. An open ear, including an uncompromising one, might take you a long way with your wanderer.

10. **Keep waiting.** Returning to God is seldom easy for a wanderer. It's sometimes equally hard to return home. For those who've never followed Christ in the first place, coming to the place of repentance and trust can take a while (like in my case). Just keep waiting, though—and return to the previous chapter

in this book about waiting if you need reminders of why waiting matters. Let the Lord renew your hope moment-by-moment and day-by-day.

11. **Keep trusting.** To be clear, God might allow your wanderer to suffer the pains of disobedience to turn him back toward Him. Sometimes, wandering is fun in the first days of the journey but agonizing in the latter ones. You might want to try to fix the situation for your wanderer so those painful days don't happen, but trust God to handle the issues at hand. He knows exactly what your loved one needs—much better than you do. Again, I need to hear these words today.

> Words for myself today: I'm naturally a fixer. But, I'm also close to an idolator when I try to fix my wanderers on my own . . . when I try to play God's part. I just need to trust Him.

12. **Keep watching.** Keep your eyes on the proverbial "driveway," always watching for glimpses of God's work around you and within the heart of your loved one (and, this "glimpse" strategy is so important that I dedicate another chapter to it later in this book).

The glimpses may not occur according to your plan—indeed, they likely will not happen on your schedule—but you never know when you'll see your wanderer on his way home.

13. **Keep praying.** I come full circle here to #1 on this list simply because prayer is both a critical part of waiting *and* the easiest thing to give up when waiting gets long. All of us need at times the reminder to go back to our knees and leave our loved ones in God's hands. He can handle the situation. In the words of my young students, "He's got it!"

Where I live in North Carolina, our kids are in year-round school. It's common to see parents wait at the bus stop for their kids to arrive in the afternoon—and it's fun to watch them connect and then walk with them down the street toward their house. Their separation may have been only a few hours, but the glee at seeing each other again is no less real.

That's my prayer for you today: that someday soon—no matter how long the wait has been—it's your loved one who gets off the bus, reconnects with you, and walks with you toward home. In the meantime, you may grieve—but keep pressing on!

Even if you watch through tears—tears that your wanderer is not yet shedding for himself or herself—join me in watching for the bus.

ACTION STEPS:

1. Identify the person(s) whose sin most grieves you. Pray for him or her.

2. Looking at the list of 13 "Keep ________ statements," mark the one you most need to seek to improve. Ask the Lord for help.

3. State for yourself (even write somewhere) the primary insight you've gained from this chapter.

CHAPTER 6

Why Prayer Matters as We Wait

In an earlier chapter, I mentioned a "son" I believed in deeply who wandered from his faith in ways I could not have imagined. I could easily talk about the decisions he made and the resulting anguish those who loved him experienced, but that's not the focus of this chapter. None of us should get so focused on the wanderer that we take our eyes off the God who pursues.

So, I want to—rather, I *need* to—turn our attention in this chapter to our prayer-answering God who welcomes our bringing our heartache to His throne. It's because He hears our cries of intercession that I can write this book in the first place. In fact, I invite you to take time right now, lay this book aside, and pray one more time. Ask God to make you both a prayer warrior and a "prayer waiter" on behalf of wanderers.

Our Hope: God Answers Prayer

I've been in places around the world where I've watched followers of other faiths pray to gods they created with their own hands, verbalizing words to statues and figurines who had ears but could not hear. I've also watched in other places as worshippers literally clapped their hands to, according to their own explanation, "make sure our gods are awake to hear us." In both cases, words that might even be heartfelt and passionate only dissipate into the air toward non-existent gods.

That's not the case with the God of the Bible, however. He welcomes us into His presence as we come to Him boldly (Heb 4:16). He hears His people when we seek Him earnestly, as this summary from my book, *The Potential and Power of Prayer*, illustrates:

> For example, it was in response to prayer that God pulled Lot out of Sodom (Genesis 18– 19); gave Hannah a child (1 Samuel 1); granted Solomon

> wisdom (2 Chronicles 1); brought fire down on the prophets of Baal (1 Kings 18); delivered Hezekiah and his people from the Assyrians (2 Kings 19); extended Hezekiah's life (2 Kings 20); granted Nehemiah favor with the king (Nehemiah 1–2); gave Zechariah and Elizabeth a son as the forerunner of Christ (Luke 1); empowered the early church with boldness (Acts 4); and freed Paul and Silas from prison (Acts 16). Given these stories and others, we cannot miss the truth that God, who established prayer as a means to accomplish his purposes, listens to us when we pray.[3]

It's all really quite amazing, actually. God hears us, and He answers us. He's a good Father who gives Himself to us (Luke 11:13)—so why would we *not* choose to take our burdens to Him? Why would we carry the weight of our wandering loved ones on our own shoulders when God can handle that weight much better than you and I can?

I have five men in my life who've been pastoral role models for me. Two are now with the Lord, but all of these lives still mark mine. These men are most remarkable followers of God, but here's one thing about them that most captures my attention: prayer drips off their lips. Spend any time with them at all, and you get the sense that they have an intimate, intensely real, almost non-stop conversation with

God going on at any given moment. That kind of prayer marks their lives because they genuinely love God and cannot imagine a day without talking to Him. And, the same God to whom they pray is the God to whom we take our wandering loved ones.

Prayer really does matter as we live . . . and as we wait.

Our Problem: We Often Try to Solve First and Pray Second

Jesus taught us something here through His actions according to Luke 5:15-16. The crowds gathered to hear Him preach His message, and the sick waited on Him to extend to them His healing power. Everybody waited in anticipation for Him to work, but here's what He did at times: He "often withdrew to the wilderness for prayer." Apparently, He left behind the work to prioritize His time with the Father; He prayed first and ministered second.

We so often do just the opposite, especially when our heart longs to see someone turn back to God. We know we need to pray—so we do it, but often only perfunctorily—even while we're figuring out our next move to convince someone to come home. I may be describing only myself, but I have a hunch that many of us are more likely to plan and ask God to bless our plans than we are to pray for God to show us His plan first.

Again, let me return briefly to *The Potential and Power of Prayer* for an illustration. As I was writing that book, here's what happened:

> I just noticed that the power supply on my laptop is getting low. I have been writing for hours, working on this chapter. My focus has been on word after word, sentence after sentence, paragraph after paragraph, and section after section. I have been "in the zone," and I have not paused to do anything else. However, my computer has been slowly dying. The power adapter is lying on the floor next to me—ready to be plugged in—but I have been so wrapped up in the task that I overlooked my waning power supply. All the while, more than sufficient power has been easily within my reach.[4]

That's the way we too often treat prayer, I'm afraid, even as we think about wandering loved ones. We have God's power at hand through prayer, but we seek other answers first. Meanwhile, we grieve . . . and worry . . . and lose heart as we look for our own solutions to reach our wanderers while God waits for us to come to Him.

A Solution: Pray First with Intentionality

Prayer matters, among other reasons, because it's a cry for God to intervene in someone's life. Moreover, it's an admission that we can't fix somebody's wandering heart. I don't want to reduce prayer to a set of formulas, but sometimes we need help developing a focused habit of prayer that matters so much as we long to reach others. For that reason, I want to propose a guided way for you to pray for your wandering loved one.

Simply stated, build your prayers around the texts describing lostness that we considered in a previous chapter. If you don't remember them, here they are with a corresponding prayer to pray for your wandering prodigal:

- **Ephesians 2:2** (NLT) – " You used to live in sin, just like the rest of the world, obeying the devil—the commander of the powers in the unseen world. He is the spirit at work in the hearts of those who refuse to obey God."

PRAYER: *"God, please give (NAME) victory over the powers in the unseen world."*

- **2 Corinthians 4:3-4** – "If the Good News we preach is hidden behind a veil, it is hidden only from people who are perishing. Satan, who is the god of this world, has blinded the minds of those who don't believe."

PRAYER: *"God, I'm asking you to open (NAME)'s blinded mind."*

- **Colossians 1:13-14** – "For he has rescued us from the kingdom of darkness and transferred us into the Kingdom of his dear Son, who purchased our freedom and forgave our sins."

PRAYER: *"God, please transfer (NAME) from the kingdom of darkness to the kingdom of Your Son."*

- **2 Timothy 2:26** – "Then they will come to their senses and escape from the devil's trap. For they have been held captive by him to do whatever he wants."

PRAYER: *"God, (NAME) is caught in the devil's trap. Please bring him to his senses, and free him."*

- **Acts 26:17b-18a** – "Yes, I am sending you [the Apostle Paul] to the Gentiles to open their eyes, so they may turn from darkness to light and from the power of Satan to God."

PRAYER: *"God, You are far more powerful than Satan. Move in (NAME)'s heart to turn to You. Send someone to be a witness to him."*

I trust you understand what I'm recommending here: let the Bible guide your intercession. I've mentioned before that I have two persons in my life for whom I've been praying for years (50+ years in one case, and 15+ years in the other). I love both of them deeply, and sometimes my emotion overwhelms me as I pray for them. At other times, the enemy tries to distract me as I pray for them. In either situation, returning to the Word and clinging to it as my prayer guide are exactly the steps I need to take.

> Words for me: "Returning to the Word and clinging to it as my prayer guide are exactly the steps I need to take."

I hope these steps will guide and encourage you, too. Indeed, I've just prayed again that all my readers, including you, will have found prayerful, praise-filled hope in this chapter.

ACTION STEPS:

1. Begin to compile a list of not only your wanderers, but also of others for whom you will intercede, knowing other believers carry the same kind of burden you likely do. Shoulder the burden with them by being on your knees alongside them.

2. Pray throughout an entire day this week for a wanderer. When you do, please remember my wanderers, too.

3. State for yourself (even write somewhere) the primary insight you've gained from this chapter.

CHAPTER 7

Watching for "Glimpses" along the Way

It's a Bible story I return to often. God's people had rebelled deeply against Him by creating and worshiping a golden calf, and God saw them as a "stubborn and rebellious people" (Exo 33:5). Prior to leading the people toward the Promised Land, Moses wanted assurance that God was going with them as He had been with them in the past. So, his request was simply for God to show him His glory—to make His presence evident again as He went before His people.

God later placed Moses in the crevice of a rock and allowed His presence to pass by him. We don't know for certain all that Moses experienced, but whatever it was was the product of the grace of God. He protected Moses with His "hand" even as He showed him His "back"—in the words of pastor and author Tony Merida, "that is, a glimpse of His glory."[5] Moses then did the only proper thing: he bowed and worshiped (Exo 34:8).

> "The glory of God isn't defined in his Word; no, his glory is so grand that it splashes across every page of his book. . . . You see, there's only One who exists in the universe who is ultimate in glory, ultimate in greatness, ultimate in beauty and ultimate in perfection, and, he is all of these things in everything he is and in everything he does."
>
> —Paul David Tripp,
> "The Doctrine of Glory"[6]

Just a glimpse of God's glory and His work will take you to your knees. In fact, it will take you to your face to worship.

Just a glimpse, too, is all we need to keep believing, keep trusting, and keep watching for God to work in the lives of wanderers.

Just one glimpse can rivet your eyes back to the end of the driveway as you wait for someone to come home.

Just a glimpse.

Why Glimpses Matter

Think about that reality in general with me for a moment, and then let's apply that thought to the focus of this book. When you start watching for just "glimpses" of God's glory and what He's up to around you, things change:

1. **You'll read the Word with more expectancy.** You will go to the Scriptures wanting to know God and His ways better. You'll want to see His hand.

2. **You will re-prioritize your life.** When you're watching for glimpses of God's glory each day, the "stuff" you're working to gain and the fame you might be seeking to get won't matter much anymore.

3. **You'll approach the day differently if you start out watching for even the "little" things God's doing.** You won't start the day with a negative heart; you'll instead start it with an excited and expectant one.

4. **You won't get distracted and discouraged by the tough times of life.** When you're seeing only the troubles, you might well miss little things God is doing around you. You need to watch for those little things every day.

5. **Especially in these chaotic days, you will find reminders of hope.** You know that life can be exhausting some days. Just a glimpse or two of God's glory, however, can revive your tired spirit.

6. **You'll deal better with the hard moments of the day.** Rather than grow hardened by these moments, you will begin to ask, "What might God be doing in this difficult situation?" He might show you His glory in unexpected ways.

7. **You will less readily give in to temptation.** When you're always watching for glimpses of God's glory, the temporary pleasure of sin loses its power.

8. **You'll pray more in gratitude.** In fact, responding to God with thanksgiving when He graciously makes Himself known to you through the glimpses is only right.

9. **You will be more amazed that you're privileged to be God's child.** The fact that the eternal Creator makes Himself known to you and has chosen to use you ought to fill you with wonder. That's more likely to happen when your eyes are always turned to Him and His work.

10. **You won't give up easily.** An attitude of defeat doesn't linger long when you're always watching and waiting for something greater: to see just a glimpse of God and His work. Glimpses renew and revive even the most hopeless person.

More specifically in terms of this book and this particular chapter, I encourage you to watch for glimpses of God's work in your loved ones for whom you've been praying so long. *Just a glimpse* that God might be up to something in their lives can refill your heart with expectation and hope.

I say it again: *just a glimpse.* That's all you need for now.

The Rest of the Story: Glimpses in My Parents' Lives

It's finally time to tell you the rest of my parents' story that I've sprinkled throughout this book. I and many others prayed for my dad for 36 years before he rather unexpectedly turned to Christ at age 71. I say "unexpectedly" because none of us knew just how strongly he was thinking about his spiritual condition until the day he called my younger brother and asked him to come talk more about Jesus.

Clearly and undeniably, my dad was ready to follow Jesus that day. So dramatically did God change Dad that he was amazingly different the last three years he lived. He became kind, loving, and giving, and he became the best Grandpa I've ever known. "Grandpa Charlie" knew Jesus in ways that nobody who knew him before his conversion could deny.

Looking back, though, I can now see glimpses I simply wasn't watching for at the time. He started initiating conversations about religion, even long before he turned from his pluralism to Christ. He went to church occasionally not to hear the gospel, but to hear his grandchildren sing. At times, he even asked me how my "church work" was going. Just a few glimpses . . . .

My mom, though she saw the obvious change in my dad, still wasn't ready to believe. She called me when Dad died and told me, "I saw a peace in his face like I've never seen in him"—but that was not enough to lead her to believe. That step would take another eleven years of our prayers—47 years altogether.

When it did happen, however, it again caught us somewhat by surprise. Mom wasn't in church when it happened. She hadn't been talking to a pastor about spiritual stuff. No, she simply called me and told me she had come to the place to trust Jesus. Both my brother and I were, frankly, a bit skeptical, but it didn't take long to see that God had performed another miracle in our family.

Mom got her first Bible and her first Bible study booklet at age 79, not long after I had the privilege of baptizing her with my brother in the baptismal waters with us. I wish I could show you the picture of her baptism I keep in my office—a picture I cherish not only because I can see my mom's joy on her face, but also because that photo says daily to me, "Don't give up on others. Don't give up on God. He's still working." It also says, "Watch for the glimpses"—as I will show you again in a moment.

I wish you could have been with me, too, when Mom called me and said, "Chuck, do you remember what I told you about the peace I saw in your dad's face when he died? Now, I can look in the mirror and see that same peace in my face!" Mom lived only six more months after her conversion, but those six months were incredibly fun as we watched our new sister in Christ flourish in a faith we often wondered if she would ever accept.

Again, though, there were glimpses. Mom, too, went to church to see her grandkids in skits and plays. Over the years, she at times went to gospel concerts with me to hear quartet music even when she'd never come to hear me preach. The spoken Word was still too much for her, but the music was a move in the right direction. Late in life, she also started giving her energies and time to help others—almost in a way to "earn" a salvation she was sure God would never just grant her. Just some glimpses . . .

The Challenge for All of Us

Here's my point in this chapter: ask God to help you see glimpses of His work in the lives of your wandering loved one. Those glimpses might be quick, sporadic, and fleeting, but watch for them. Keep your eyes open for an unexpected willingness to have a short conversation . . . a surprising request for prayer . . . an "out of the blue" comment or question about church . . . a Christian book on the table . . . a softening heart toward family members . . . a willingness to come home for a holiday . . . or just a kind word to you in general or an affirming comment about a Christ-follower. These glimpses may be just that for now—only glimpses—but that's all you need right now to keep praying.

> "I want to see God doing great things in my sister's life, but I've learned to rejoice over the little things I see. Even one little thing changes my perspective, at least for a little while."
>
> —a praying brother

Even if you are not in a healthy relationship with your wanderer, pray that *somebody* will see those glimpses. Ask God to give you faith that says, "I don't need to see the glimpse to trust that it's there somewhere. Let somebody see it, Father. Let *somebody* see it even if I'm not that somebody."

Just a glimpse.

Ask God to let you and me see one today.

Then, let's watch with expectant eyes.

ACTION STEPS:

1. Pray that God will show you glimpses of His work today.

2. Watch for those glimpses—and praise God when you see them!

3. State for yourself (even write somewhere) the primary insight you've gained from this chapter.

CHAPTER 8

Learning to Love when Loving a Wanderer is Hard

I talk regularly with parents, grandparents, and others who desperately long for someone in their family to follow Jesus. Their grief is sometimes almost agonizing, especially if they've been praying for years . . . or decades even, like I and others prayed for my parents. Love compels you to pray and keep on praying even as you wait, but the waiting can seem unbearable at times.

It's also love that wounds grieving parents when adult children choose to walk away from the faith of their childhood. Everything seemed to go smoothly as they raised their kids . . . until those kids became adults themselves who quickly departed from the faith of their mothers and fathers.

Sometimes, in fact, wanderers become almost unlovable in their rebellion. Love gets hard for those waiting and watching, especially if their loved one is a young adult still living at home but rejecting that home's values. It's hard, too, when the rebellion is an ongoing lifestyle assault against the Christian faith. Love's also tough when the wanderer has seemingly disappeared in an intentional move to the faraway country of the prodigal son.

Back to the Prodigal Son

I realize again that the point of the parable of the prodigal son in Luke 15 is not about his journey, but his story nevertheless has caused me to think about different stages of life—especially as I pray for and seek to reach wandering people I love:

1. **The stage of youthful arrogance.** The son was so enamored with what life still had ahead of him that he simply wanted to have his money now, run with it, and experience all that he perceived life offered him. And, I suspect there's a reason Jesus painted him as traveling to a faraway country—to a place far from responsibility, accountability, and family teachings.

How painful it is to watch someone you love begin to move away from his or her upbringing, apparently finding fun and excitement outside your family and disconnected from your family's teachings. Sometimes, in fact, you can watch a loved one begin to create that distance even while living in your home—and it's tough to know best how to love and confront that wanderer-to-be.

Maybe these words just described your situation; if so, know that I paused to pray for you and others as I wrote those words (and, I hope, you are encouraged by how many times I've prayed for you and your wanderer long before you read these words).

2. **The stage of "wild living" (Luke 15:13, NLT).** The best we know about the younger brother's reckless spending habits is that his older brother accused him of turning to prostitutes (Luke 15:30). Our own stories were likely different, but I suspect some of us can talk about days when we, too, wasted our energy, our dollars, our time, our training, and even our relationships on dumb choices that seemed "cool" at the time (sorry for language that dates me for what I am: old). What mattered most to us was the fun the world advertised so strongly that we didn't want

to miss out—so we wasted our money chasing more and more fun that would never ultimately bring us peace.

My experience is that this stage is often the most painful one for parents and others who know only that their wanderer is somewhere living a life displeasing to God. Distance only compounds the pain, and sometimes the pain becomes anger and numbness at the same time. Faith gets stretched to its limit.

3. **The stage of painful recognition.** The portrayal of the prodigal son in Luke 15 is gripping. How far he fell from spending his wealth to eating among the pigs! Pleasure rolled into famine, wealth into poverty, and riotous living into aloneness. He came to this point when he realized the hard way that his poor choices had cost him more than they brought him. They seemed fun at the time, but they hardly gave him any sense of lasting joy. He found himself hungry, embarrassed, and far away from home. It's both a bad place to be and a good place to be at the same time when shame turns to repentance and return.

   Love can be really tough at this stage, especially if we have the opportunity to try to save our wanderers from the pain I've described above. If we always seek to rescue them, though, they may never come to the end of themselves as is often necessary for them to turn toward home. Knowing how to love wanderers isn't always easy when we want to save them from themselves.

> "I'm naturally a rescuer. When I forget that tendency, I fear I get in the way of my son's feeling the foolishness of his choices. Honestly, it's hard for me to get out of the way."
>
> —a parent still watching . . . and learning

4. **The stage of gracious homecoming.** It's hard to put into words what this stage means. In the parable of Luke 15, the father threw a party and celebrated his son's return (actions that frustrated the older, Pharisee-like brother in the field). We sometimes need the reminder that our heavenly Father stands waiting and watching for wanderers, and He welcomes them with open arms on their return. That day brings rejoicing even "in the presence of God's angels" (Luke 15:10).

Our love for wandering ones is likely most powerful when we realize just how deep the Father's love is for each of us—and just how little any of us deserves it. We were all hard-to-love wanderers at some point, and only the undeserved love and grace of God allowed us to celebrate on the day of our own return. That same grace has a way of melting our hearts for even the most unlovable wanderers. In God's love, we can love them with wisdom, patience, and persistence. In His grace and according to His timing, we can also plan a party someday.

Loving when It's Tough to Love

Waiting for wandering loved ones to turn to God is so common these days that many folks have written about walking this path.[7] Based on these writings, conversations with waiting parents and grandparents, and my own actions toward my wanderers who sometimes frustrate me, here are some simple ways to keep on loving wanderers when they're not so lovable:

1. **Fast once a week on behalf of your wanderer.** Years ago, a pastor friend told me that he and his wife began to take that step when one of their children had gone astray. They fasted and prayed every Friday

for years until the young man came home—and they became so committed to that practice that they still do it every week for all their children and grandchildren even if they've remained faithful to God. As I write this chapter, in fact, I'm fasting on behalf of the two wanderers I'm pleading with God to grab.

2. **Keep the door open to conversations.** One of my fathers in the faith once said to me when I was moving away to start a new ministry, "Know that our porchlight is always on for you." Leave the porchlight on for your wanderer, and make sure he or she knows it's always on. Pray your wanderer will remember those words at the right time.

> "Know that without a relationship there is no influence. So, if you want to maintain a redemptive influence, you must do your best to maintain a relationship."
>
> —a "porchlight" perspective
> from a father who's been there

3. **Learn about your wanderer's world.** You can at times ask questions, meet friends, and spend time with your wanderer without compromising your gospel witness. One father I know not only stayed in touch with his struggling daughter, but he also maintained his commitment to have daddy/daughter dates even when she was wandering. Another set of parents I know intentionally made efforts to get to know their wandering daughter's friends—some who themselves were wanderers from their own family and faith. In both cases, a willingness to try to understand a daughter and her world made a difference.

4. **Learn to listen, ideally simply to hear without taking personally any hurtful words you hear.** Do your best to find something you can affirm in a conversation with your wanderer. Try to avoid quick, impulsive responses that only foster division. I actually whisper under my breath sometimes, "Lord, don't let me respond wrongly" when I get the sense that a conversation with my wandering loved one is going awry. I've learned the hard way that I sometimes should be quiet and later take my heartache to the Lord; for now, I just need to do my best to listen.

5. **Trust God's Spirit to give you wisdom about when and how to speak truth to your wanderer.** One assumption I'm making as I write this book is that you, my reader, read God's Word and seek Him in prayer. If that's not the case, I first challenge you to get your own heart right with the Lord if you want Him to intercept your loved one's wanderings. If your heart is where the Lord wants you to be, however, ask God to give you wisdom in conversations with your loved one. Trust that He will show you when and how to speak truth as you walk faithfully with Him.

6. **Keep running to God with your heartache and frustrations.** Just as quickly and as hard as your wanderer might be running *from* God, you keep running *to* Him. His arms are big. His shoulders are broad. He can handle whatever you bring to Him. And, He can renew your love for your sometimes unlovable wanderer in the process.

All the while, keep trusting. Don't give up.

That's the point of this book.

ACTION STEPS:

1. Decide what step(s) you need to take to love your wanderer even if he or she is unlovable.

2. Prayerfully take one of those steps.

3. State for yourself (even write somewhere) the primary insight you've gained from this chapter.

CHAPTER 9

Watching for Opportunities to Speak the Gospel

Let's do a quick review as we press toward the end of this book. Remember that I'm using the word "wanderer" in this book to refer not only to those who've walked away from their faith, but also for those who've simply never responded positively to the gospel despite years of witness. In both cases, somebody's wandering from the things of God.

And, in both cases, somebody needs to hear the gospel—just like my parents did and the folks for whom I'm praying today still do. Apart from the gospel, there can be no hope.

My goal in this chapter is to tell you more about my parents' journey as I also offer you practical steps for seeking God, pursuing your wandering loved ones, and looking for open doors to speak the gospel with them at the same time. At the end of the day, it's speaking the good news at the appropriate time and praying wanderers will hear it in that moment that will make the difference. As you read the rest of this chapter, consider which of these steps you need to take:

1. **Just keep praying.** I suspect you're not surprised that I start here. In my *Potential and Power of Prayer* book, I describe prayer as "a cry for relationship with God and a confession of dependence on Him."[8] On one hand, prayer says, "God, I love You"; on the other, it says, "God, I need You." Prayer of behalf of wanderers says both: "God, I love you, and I want them to love you, too—but I cannot change their hearts. I'm completely dependent on You to do that."

   The challenge for me sometimes is to not allow my heart to become hardened while waiting decades for God to answer my prayers. I'm grateful the Lord continues to teach me these words: "I love you, and I love your wanderer. Don't quit now. Just keep praying."

> "We have yet to see the change we long for in our daughter, but we've changed. We are no longer frantic and afraid, but we are resting against his bosom like a weaned child, knowing that God will accomplish all things concerning us; knowing that God also grieves for our precious daughter, and in his time, he will win her heart. God is good and does all things well, and in this I will rest until the prodigal returns and the feasting begins."
>
> —a trusting mother

2. **Get others to pray with you for your loved ones.** In my various roles as pastor, professor, and missionary trainer, I've had opportunities for many years to travel all over North America and around the globe. Early in these roles—as I've already mentioned in this book—I made a commitment to ask believers everywhere to pray for my parents. I made that request through translators at times, but I can't recall ever missing an opportunity to gather prayer warriors around me on behalf of Mom and Dad. I can still envision in my mind and hear in my ears the prayers from different peoples, living in numerous countries,

representing multiple generations, speaking in various languages, lifting my parents to the Lord.

When my parents did turn to the Lord, I'm convinced God responded to the prayers of generations of believers. In fact, I delighted when folks who had been praying with me for decades rejoiced with me, too. Perhaps you don't have the same access to believers around the globe that I've had, but you do have other believers you can intentionally invite to join you in intercession for your loved ones. Just start asking today.

3. **With other prayer partners interceding with you, ask God to give you *and/or others* opportunities to speak truth into your loved ones' lives.** I remind you again that the apostle Paul asked for prayer that he might speak the gospel boldly and clearly and that God might give him an open door to speak to others (Eph 6:18-20, Col 4:2-4). You and I need the same kind of undergirding—especially when we're watching for open doors to speak to wandering loved ones. We need courage to speak that comes from Holy Spirit-empowering through the prayers of God's people.

After Pam and I moved from Ohio where my parents lived, we knew our opportunities to influence them would be fewer. Increasing geographical distance separated us and pushed us to pray for others to be witnesses to them. My brother and his family lived near them, and it was primarily they who led my parents to the Lord. I was a professor of evangelism at the time, but it was others who did the evangelistic work in my parents' lives. *Who* did the gospel witness didn't matter, though; what mattered was that God used *someone* to do it. Begin praying today for someone to speak gospel truth to your loved one.

4. **If you have opportunity, tell your wandering loved one your own gospel story.** I'm often struck by how seldom children and grandchildren (including adults) know the gospel stories of their parents and grandparents. They don't know how their family members first heard the gospel, nor do they know their baptism stories. Little do they know that even their own parents and grandparents may have struggled at times in following God faithfully and fully. As far as some wanderers know, nobody else in their family has ever walked their wayward path. That simply may not be the case.

May I make a suggestion to you? Do your best to make sure that not only your wandering loved ones hear your full gospel story, but that others in your family, small group, and congregation hear it as well. Think *humility* as you speak to your wanderer, perhaps with a simple request like, "You know, it occurs to me that I've never told you my whole faith story. I don't know if you'd be interested, but could I take a few minutes and tell you about my own journey? You might even find that our stories overlap a bit." You never know—maybe your wandering loved one will be okay with a conversation that could help him or her understand you *and* God better.

> "I've learned, too, that some people will read a handwritten note when they wouldn't be willing to talk directly. A note's just more personal than some electronic means to communicate. Maybe that's an option, too, to reach out to a wanderer and tell your story."
>
> —a Christian leader and father of a wanderer who's used this strategy often

5. **Trust that God's working even when you cannot see what He's doing.** I mentioned this Bible story

earlier, but I regularly remind myself of the story of Jairus in Mark 5. Jairus, a ruler of the synagogue, had asked Jesus to come heal his dying daughter, but Jesus did not get there in time. The daughter died. Still, Jesus told the dad to let go of his fear and just believe (Mark 5:36). All the evidence from a human perspective said the story was over, but Jesus knew better. He knew God was still up to something—though Jairus would not know what He was doing until the miracle of resurrection had later taken place. Sometimes we see God's hand more retroactively after He works than we did when we were wrestling with His silence in the present.

Neither of my parents first made their profession of faith in the context of a church worship service. We had prayed for them and invited them to church for years, but it was not in a "response time" at the end of a service that they first prayed for forgiveness. As a reminder, my dad called my brother to talk about Jesus, and my mom simply informed us that she had sought God's grace and forgiveness when she realized that God would, in fact, forgive her. She didn't know all the proper terminology, but she knew God had changed her heart.

In both cases, God had been working even though we did not know it at the time. More than once since then, I've told folks that God reminded me of this truth through the conversion of my parents: *"When God's doing His work, He's under no obligation to let us in on the details."* He's God, and we're not—and our responsibility is to keep trusting Him even in His seeming silence. I offer this same truth to you even as I remind myself about it as I write these words.

6. **Don't let the enemy rob you of hope when he aims his arrows of doubt at you.** My older sister is the one remaining immediate family member who has not yet followed Christ. I've also told you about another buddy who is like a son to me who has turned fully from his faith. Today, in fact, my heart breaks for them in deep, painful, gripping ways. Given the stories of my parents' dramatic conversions—not to mention my younger brother's prior transformation through grace and corresponding freedom from addictions—you would think I would always, always trust God's hand in the lives of people I love. Even, I, though, face the enemy's attacks of discouragement and doubt at times. It seems Satan and his forces want us to ignore yesterday's powerful victories in the midst of today's faith struggles.

That's when I remember these truths that have meant so much to me over the years:

- God is God. He just is. And, He always will be.
- God has already disarmed the powers through Jesus' death on the cross (Col 2:15).
- God is still drawing to Himself a people (Rev 7:9).
- God loves my loved ones much more than I do.
- God still hears prayers.
- God doesn't have to show me what He's doing.
- God still calls me to trust Him—and He's still trustworthy.

> Even those of us who've seen God redeem wanderers in the past must regularly remember these truths above. That's why this book is for me as much as it is for you.

7. **Keep praying some more.** You've now heard words similar to these several times in this book. That's intentional, of course, because it's God who calls, pursues, saves, and sanctifies. Apart from Him, you and I can do nothing for ourselves or for others. Don't give up on prayer even as you watch for opportunities to speak the gospel to your wandering loved one.

ACTION STEPS:

1. Write out your Christian testimony, and share it with someone in your family.

2. Ask God to give you opportunities to share it with your wandering loved one.

3. State for yourself (even write somewhere) the primary insight you've gained from this chapter.

CHAPTER 10

Three More Challenges

Let me start this final chapter with a caveat. This first part of this conclusion might, upon your first read, be tough to read at points. After I've done my best throughout this book to offer you hope if you have a wandering loved one, you might not expect the first part of this chapter . . . . but, I'm asking you, friend, to listen closely to my words as you keep reading. I trust these words, too, will be hopeful.

I want you trusting God, always standing at the end of driveway as you watch and believe that He will draw your wanderer back. I'm trusting that's the case for my wanderers. If I did not have that hope, in fact, I'm not sure how my heart would carry this burden. I must cling to the heart and the hands of God even as I wait for Him to work.

You, too, must cling.

We cannot give up. Keep reading with that truth in mind.

Trust God for the Future

In the famous "faith chapter" of Hebrews 11, the writer records these words about some of the patriarchs from the book of Genesis:

> It was by faith that Isaac promised blessings for the future to his sons, Jacob and Esau.
>
> It was by faith that Jacob, when he was old and dying, blessed each of Joseph's sons and bowed in worship as he leaned on his staff.
>
> It was by faith that Joseph, when he was about to die, said confidently that the people of Israel would leave Egypt. He even commanded them to take his bones with them when they left. (Heb 11:20-22)

If you look closely at these words, I want you to see the faith of these men. For example, Isaac, who himself was

God's promised son to Abraham—the one through whom would come the people of God (Gen 12:1-3)—trusted that God was going to bless his own sons, Jacob and Esau, *in the future.*

Years later, when Jacob himself was old and dying, he blessed Joseph's sons—trusting that God would honor that request *in the days to come.*

Then Joseph, when he himself was about to leave this earth, commanded the leaders of God's people to make sure they would take his bones back to Israel when they left Egypt. The elderly Joseph was dying, but he died in complete confidence that God was going to accomplish His plan *whenever He wanted to do so.*

For all these heroes of the faith, their present-tense faith gave them undying future-tense hope—even a hope they carried with them into eternity.

That's where I want to start this chapter. My prayer for all of us is that God would bring back our wanderers during our lifetimes so we could rejoice and celebrate with them upon their return. I want all of us to have opportunities to throw a big party like the father of the prodigal son in Luke 15 did. I want us, in fact, to see God work in such a way that we must start getting the party supplies together today—and I'm always going to pray that way. Always.

What I've come to realize, though, is that God does not always answer our prayers while we're living. Sometimes He calls us home ahead of time, and we die at the end of the driveway, still watching and believing. Our time in this world ends without our having yet seen our wanderer coming around the corner. That possibility, though, *does not take away our reasons for trusting our wanderers to God.*

He who is sovereign over the plan for our lives is also sovereign over the lives of our wanderers. The timing for our departure is in His hands, and so is the timing for our wanderers to come running home. Should the latter happen after we've gone to heaven, that's okay. We'll have all eternity to hear the rest of the story and celebrate homecomings like we never could have in this world.

In the meantime, we keep praying, loving, and trusting.

And, we keep watching for glimpses . . . .

Stay in the Word, and Encourage Others

I first considered writing this book because of my joy of seeing my parents come to the Lord after decades of prayer. I wanted others to experience the sweet peace that comes when God finally answers prayers and dramatically changes lives.

Then, the burden for working on this resource grew as I heard the hurting hearts of believers who struggled still trusting God on behalf of others after years of heartfelt prayer with apparently no answer. I, too, am waiting on some of those answers even as I bring this book toward a close. I'm writing to encourage my heart as well as yours.

And, I want to challenge you, reader, to be an encourager of others walking in your "waiting" shoes as all of us journey together. These folks watching for wanderers are all around us. Some are quite open about their heartache, but others carry their burdens silently and alone. They weep in their prayer closet but smile in their small group. Ask God to make you sensitive to all these folks so you might walk together. Somehow, two people carrying similar burdens together makes the burden a bit lighter.

As you read the scriptures, watch for words like these that call you to seek our God—a God filled with prayer-answering love:

- Search for the Lord and for his strength; continually seek him. (Psa 105:4)
- The LORD is close to all who call on him, yes, to all who call on him in truth. (Psa 145:18)
- Seek the LORD while you can find him. Call on him now while he is near. (Isa 55:6)
- If you look for me wholeheartedly, you will find me. (Jer 2913)
- Come to me, all of you who are weary and carry heavy burdens, and I will give you rest. (Matt 11:28)
- Let us come boldly to the throne of our gracious God. There we will receive his mercy, and we will find grace to help us when we need it most. (Heb 4:16)
- Come close to God, and God will come close to you. (James 4:8)

> "Remember that prayer is the most impactful spiritual investment as you shepherd your own heart and love well the one who is struggling."
>
> —a parent who has seen victory in a wanderer's life

Then, as you seek God through His Word, watch as you read for calls to wait and trust, like these texts from the book of Psalms:

- Wait patiently for the Lord. Be brave and courageous. Yes, wait patiently for the Lord. (Psa 27:14)
- Be still in the presence of the Lord, and wait patiently for him to act. (Psa 37:7)
- For I am waiting for you, O Lord. You must answer for me, O Lord my God. (Psa 38:15)
- I waited patiently for the Lord to help me, and he turned to me and heard my cry. (Psa 40:1)

- I wait for the Lord; I wait and put my hope in his word. I wait for the Lord more than watchmen for the morning—more than watchmen for the morning. (Psa 130:5-6)

Today, let the Word of God saturate your heart. Seek Him. Wait for Him. Trust Him. Be prayerful in your spirit, persistent in your hope, patient in your trust, and praise-filled with your words. Watch for the Lord to work in your wandering loved one's life according to His time schedule.

Keep Praying, Even for Those Who Have Not Wandered, and Lean on Your Own Prayer Warriors

I've mentioned this responsibility before in this book, but I want to remind you of it one more time. You may have loved ones who are walking with the Lord today. They're faithful. They're committed. They're an example to others. They so love the Lord that you delight in their Christian witness.

But, they're also in a spiritual battle.

They're up against an enemy who wants to lure them, too, into the far fields of wandering.

Start today to pray that the world would never grab their attention. Pray proactively that they would remain faithful and raise up other generations who do the same. Don't wait until your loved one becomes a wanderer to start praying.

Finally, make sure you have prayer partners interceding for you *so that yourself don't become a wanderer*. Get some folks who've "got your back" as you serve the Lord in a chaotic world. Ask them to stay on their knees on your behalf even as you keep praying for others who've wandered. Then, keep your eyes on Jesus and run your race faithfully (Heb 12:1-2) so even wanderers see something genuine and life-giving in you.

ACTION STEPS:

1. Spend some time talking to God about how you want to trust Him for the future, even if He does not answer your prayers in this lifetime. Seek Him in prayer even as you wait.

2. Enlist 2-3 prayer warriors who will pray that you never wander, either. You might even give them a copy of this book to help them see the importance of their role in your life.

3. State for yourself (even write somewhere) the primary insight you've gained from this chapter..

Conclusion

Well, we've come to the end of this book. I end this writing still burdened about wanderers in my life, but even more filled with joy as I think about how faithful God has been to me and others. He heard the prayers of many for my mom and dad. He's heard the intercession for other sons in the faith who've gone astray. He's still listening and working as I pray for the wanderers in my life today. No matter how long the wait is for their return, I cannot give up.

I must not give up.

Nor should you give up as you think about the wanderers in your life.

I am praying with you that God will bring our wanderers home. Indeed, let me pray for you now:

"Father, I'm so thankful that You hear our prayers, restore our hope, and call us to You. Thank You for the brothers and sisters reading this book right

now. I pray you would grant them faith to believe and patience to wait as You work in the lives of those they love. We look forward, God, to seeing our wanderers come home. In Jesus' name and for His glory we give You these requests. Amen."

Together, friend, let's prayerfully wait at the end of the driveway. Giving up is not an option.

Endnotes

Chapter 3

[1] Chuck Lawless, *Nobodies for Jesus* (Rainer Publishing).
[2] Chuck Lawless, *The Battle Is Not Mine: Lessons I've Learned about Spiritual Warfare* (p. 18). Kindle Edition.

Chapter 6

[3] Chuck Lawless, *The Potential and Power of Prayer: How to Unleash the Praying Church* (Church Answers Resources) (p. 36). Kindle Edition.
[4] Ibid., 65.

Chapter 7

[5] Tony Merida, *Exalting Jesus in Exodus* (Christ-Centered Exposition Commentary) (p. 211). Kindle Edition.
[6] Paul David Tripp, "The Doctrine of Glory."
Link: https://www.paultripp.com/articles/posts/the-doctrine-of-glory-article

CHAPTER 8

[7] See, for example, Ivan Mesa, ed., *Before You Lose Your Faith* (Gospel Coalition, 2021); Alisa Childers and Tim Barnett *The Deconstruction of Christianity* (Tyndale, 2024).

CHAPTER 9

[8] Chuck Lawless, *The Potential and Power of Prayer: How to Unleash the Praying Church* (Church Answers Resources) (p. 25). Tyndale House Publishers. Kindle Edition.

www.ingramcontent.com/pod-product-compliance
Lightning Source LLC
La Vergne TN
LVHW090531110826
845146LV00003B/1054

* 9 7 9 8 9 9 5 4 0 3 4 1 8 *